GREAT SAND DUNES NATIONAL MONUMENT

A TRUE BOOK

by
David Petersen

Children's Press®
A Division of Grolier Publishing

New York London Hong Kong Sydney
Danbury, Connecticut

Trees worn by
blowing sand

Content Consultant
Kathy Brown
*Chief of Interpretation
Great Sand Dunes
National Monument*

Reading Consultant
Linda Cornwell
*Coordinator of School Quality
and Improvement
Indiana State Teachers
Association*

Visit Children's Press® on the
Internet at:
http://publishing.grolier.com

Library of Congress Cataloging-in-Publication Data

Petersen, David, 1946-.
    Great Sand Dunes National Monument / by David Petersen.
        p.   cm. — (A True Book)
    Includes bibliographical references and index.
    Summary: Describes the history, landscape, wildlife, and available
    activities of Great Sand Dunes National Monument.
    ISBN: 0-516-20943-4 (lib. bdg.)   0-516-26763-9 (pbk.)
    1.—Juvenile literature.   [1. 2..]   I. Title.   II. Series.
F782.G78P48   1999
917.88'49—dc21   98-42466
                                                                          CIP
                                                                          AC

© 1999 Children's Press®
A Division of Grolier Publishing Co., Inc.
All rights reserved. Published simultaneously in Canada.
Printed in the United States of America.
1 2 3 4 5 6 7 8 9 10 R 08 07 06 05 04 03 02 01 00 99

Contents

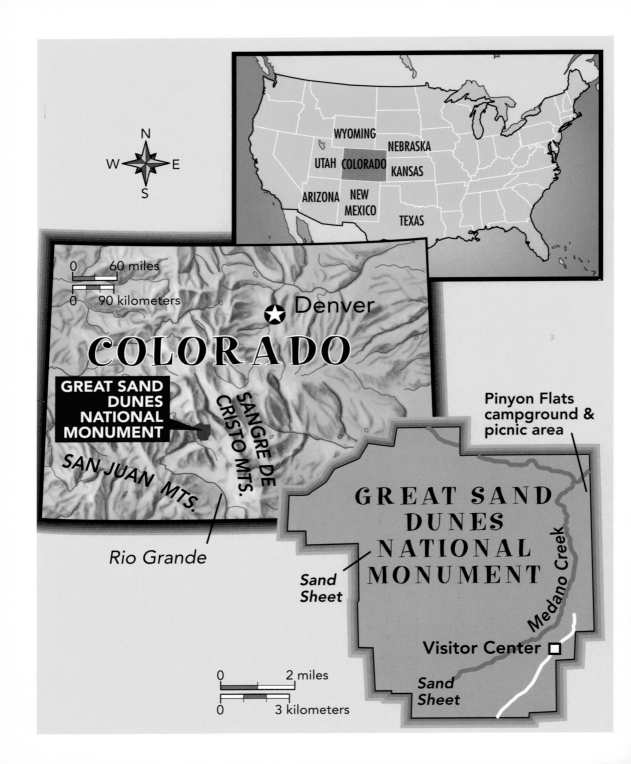

WYOMING

NEBRASKA

UTAH COLORADO

KANSAS

ARIZONA NEW
MEXICO

TEXAS

N
W E
S

0   60 miles

0   90 kilometers

☆ Denver

COLORADO

GREAT SAND
DUNES
NATIONAL
MONUMENT

SANGRE DE CRISTO MTS.

SAN JUAN MTS.

Rio Grande

Pinyon Flats
campground &
picnic area

GREAT SAND
DUNES
NATIONAL
MONUMENT

Sand
Sheet

Medano Creek

Visitor Center ☐

Sand
Sheet

0   2 miles

0   3 kilometers

America's Biggest Sandbox

If you think you're too old to play in a sandbox, you haven't been to Great Sand Dunes National Monument in Colorado.

Tucked into a corner of a high mountain valley, the Great Sand Dunes spread across 39 square miles (101 square kilometers). The dunes resemble storm-tossed waves, and crest 700 feet (214 meters) above the valley floor. These are the tallest sand dunes in North America.

Kids are especially welcome at Great Sand Dunes National Monument. They are invited to "climb on the dunes, play in the sand, splash in the creek, and have a lot of fun!"

GREAT SAND DUNES
NATIONAL MONUMENT

NATIONAL PARK SERVICE
DEPARTMENT OF THE INTERIOR

Entrance to the park

In addition to the dunes, there's a visitor center, picnic area, campground, hiking trails, rushing creeks, and snow-capped mountains with leaping wildlife.

A Monument to Contrast

The Great Sand Dunes are hidden away in the San Luis Valley of south-central Colorado. The San Luis Valley is big—nearly three times the size of the state of Delaware. It's also high—8,000 feet (2,440 m) above sea level. And across the valley's floor

The San Juan mountain range (above) and the Sangre de Cristo mountains (right)

winds the Rio Grande
(Spanish for "Big River").
Sixty miles (96 km) west of
the dunes loom the San Juan

Mountains. On the east, rising like a wall behind the dunes, is the Sangre de Cristo range. Many peaks in both ranges pierce the clouds with elevations of more than 14,000 feet (4,270 m).

In Spanish, San Juan means "Saint John." Sangre de Cristo means "Blood of Christ." The mountains, the valley, the river, and many other local features were named by early Spanish explorers.

Dune Makers

From a distance, the Great Sand Dunes resemble a huge, fan-shaped pile of sand swept into a corner by a giant broom. In fact, that's just what happened, with wind acting as the broom.

Sand, water, wind, and time: These are the dune makers.

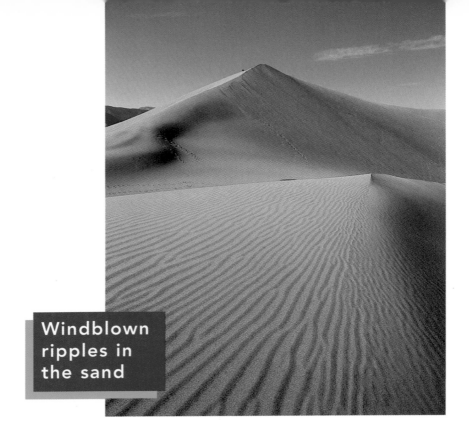

Windblown ripples in the sand

First came the Rocky Mountains, formed seventy million years ago. Movements in the earth's crust caused the land to buckle up in a long, jagged line.

Fiery lava explodes from a volcano.

About 25 million years ago, volcanoes erupted. They created the San Juan Mountains by depositing millions of tons of lava and ash.

More time passed. Ice Ages came and went, and great mountain glaciers (large

A glacier (left) washes down from snowy mountain peaks. The Rio Grande (right) winds a narrow path in the San Luis Valley.

bodies of ice) formed. The glaciers slid downhill, grinding volcanic rock into sand as they went. Swift mountain streams helped the erosion by washing tons of sand down to the Rio

Grande year after year. This still happens today.

The flow of the Rio Grande helped to spread the sand all across the valley floor. Seasonal flooding and a gradual shift of the river's channel toward the south helped, too. Strong winds, blowing from the southwest, swept the sand into the northeast corner of the valley. There, it was trapped by the Sangre de Cristo Mountains. As the sand piled ever higher, over hundreds of years, the

Great Sand Dunes were formed.

This "sweeping" process continues today. You can see it in the ripples on the faces of the dunes, and in the wind-blown cornices along their tops. These surface features change all the time as wind whips the loose sand to and fro. But the dunes themselves are stable (remain the same).

The dunes don't change, in part because of their high mois-ture content. On the surface,

Sandy patterns decorate the changeless dunes.

the sand is dry and loose. But inside the dunes, moisture from rain and melted snow binds the sand grains together.

Storm winds passing over the Sangre de Cristos from the north and east, also help to anchor (hold in place) the dunes.

A stormy sky darkens the valley.

Finally, Medano Creek flows out of the Sangre de Cristos and along the eastern edge of the dunes. Medano Creek serves as a liquid sand trap, keeping the dunes from migrating beyond.

Let's Go Dune Diving

Your first stop at Great Sand Dunes should be the monument visitor center. Browse the books and gifts. Watch a film about the dunes. View the educational displays. Step out the back door for a spectacular view of the dunes and surrounding scenery.

19

Any questions? Park rangers are experts on dune life.

And before you leave, ask a park ranger about guided nature hikes, campfire talks, the Junior Ranger Program, and other special activities for kids.

A short drive from the visitor center leads to a parking and picnic area. From there, the dunes stand like Egyptian pyramids just beyond Medano Creek. The creek is shallow and swift, with no mud or quick-sand. There are also no bridges—so leap right in!

While you're splashing across Medano Creek to the dunes, notice the "surging waves." As sand washes along the bottom of the creek, it forms small ridges—just like the wind-ripples on the dunes. Small "standing" waves form on the water's surface as it flows over the ridges. Every few seconds,

Ridges at the bottom of Medano Creek

the sand ridges grow too big and collapse, causing the standing waves to surge (rise and fall actively) forward.

After crossing Medano Creek, it's great fun to climb to the top of the nearest dune. First take a running leap off the edge and then go rolling and tumbling down—you're dune diving! The sand is gritty, but it's clean.

The only dangers on the dunes are hot sand and light-ning. The sun-warmed sand

Dive in! Dune diving is a favorite sport of young visitors to the park.

can be hot, so be sure to bring along some shoes. And standing atop a dune is no place to be during an electrical storm. You could become a human lightning rod! If you see a storm coming, get off the dunes until it passes.

Camping and Hiking

Like the picnic area, Pinyon Flats campground is just across Medano Creek from the dunes. Each campsite has a table, a fire grate, and shade trees. Water and rest rooms are nearby.

For a real adventure in camping, get a free backpacking permit and backpack to one

Hikers explore the strange dune landscape.

of several backcountry camp-sites scattered throughout the monument. Or wander off into the dunes and pitch your tent in the sand!

There are no trails among the dunes. There are other trails that lead out across the grasslands and up into the pine and aspen forests of the Sangre de Cristos.

High above the dunes, aspen and pine trees cover the hills.

Dune Life

A giant pile of sand is not a friendly environment. Yet, a few hardy plants and animals do survive in the dunes. And many more live in the surrounding grasslands, brushy foothills, and mountain forests.

In low, quiet pockets between dunes grow four

Please don't pick the sunflowers!

hardy plants that need little water: Indian ricegrass, blowout grass, scurfy pea, and yellow prairie sunflowers. Rabbit brush grows on the surrounding "sand sheet."

Dune

Great Sand Dunes tiger beetle

Living in these pockets of green are two insects found nowhere else on earth: the Great Sand Dunes tiger beetle, and a local species of circus beetle. The giant sand treader camel cricket also makes its home here.

The camel cricket got its name from its hump-backed appearance. It is wingless and makes no sound. Sand crickets spend the day buried under the sand and come out at night to

Bugs

feed. The tiger bee-
tle does not have to
leave its burrow to
catch its prey. It remains attached to the
burrow wall with a hooklike spine on its
abdomen. The beetle then waits for dinner
to crawl by and pulls it right through
the
front
door.

Sand cricket

Camel cricket

Those mouselike footprints
you see crossing the dunes
were left by kangaroo rats.
These small, long-tailed creatures are the camels of the
rodent family. Kangaroo rats

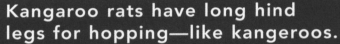

Kangaroo rats have long hind
legs for hopping—like kangeroos.

are creatures perfectly suited for desert life because they never have to drink. They get the moisture they need from their diet of seeds.

Beyond the dunes, among the grass, brush, and trees, there's a lively variety of animals. These include mountain lions, coyotes, cottontail rabbits, and chipmunks. You will find mule deer throughout the monument. Some are not the least bit shy—but never

Pronghorn (above) and mule deer (right) roam the park.

approach or feed any wild animal, small or large.

Far out on the grasslands bordering the dunes, you may see deer-size animals with white rumps. These are pronghorn—the fastest long-distance runners in the world. They live only on the open prairies of the American West.

Mammals of the San Juan and Sangre de Cristo Mountains include bighorn sheep, elk, cougars, and black bears.

Bring binoculars and check the treetops for ravens (left) and owls.

The trees and skies above the dunes are home to blue-black ravens and colorful magpies, plus a lovely variety of song-birds. And you might see owls, hawks, falcons, and golden eagles.

Poisonous snakes? Not here.

Human Visitors . . .Yesterday and Tomorrow

Humans have occupied the San Luis Valley for more than eleven thousand years. Among the first were the Clovis people, who used spears to hunt mammoths and other giant Ice Age mammals.

Next came the Folsom culture. These Stone Age people lived

Campsite of the ancient Folsom
people, outside the park

a life of total freedom, hunting
bison and gathering edible

plants. One Folsom campsite, more than ten thousand years old, is located just west of the monument entrance.

Today, the San Luis Valley remains filled with farms and ranches. There are several small towns, but no cities.

Throughout this long history of human occupation—Indian, Spanish, Mexican, and American—the sand dunes have served as a famous local landmark and natural curiosity.

The Ute

A Ute Native American couple

About six hundred years ago, Ute Indians wandered into the San Luis Valley. In the 1600s, settlers from Mexico began to arrive. And in the early 1800s, Americans came pouring in. In 1863, the remaining Utes were forced from the valley.

Marking the long Ute occupation of the Great Sand Dune area are ponderosa pine trees. These trees wear scars where big slabs of bark were removed.

Ute war chief
and teepees

The Indians used the soft, sweet, inner bark for food and medicine. One Ute-scarred tree trunk is preserved at the visitor center. Hiking trails lead to many others, hundreds of years old and still thriving.

A ponderosa pine tree peeled by the Ute

To preserve this treasure for
your enjoyment, Great Sand

The great sand dunes seem
like another world.

Dunes National Monument was established by President Herbert Hoover in 1932.

Great Sand Dunes is a National Park Service site, so all resources—wildlife, wildflowers, and sand—are protected. This means everything must stay the way the visitor finds it. When you come to visit, these greatest of all sand dunes will be waiting, looking much as they did to the first humans who ever saw them.

To Find Out More

Here are some additional resources to help you learn more about Great Sand Dunes National Park:

 **Books**

Flanagan, Alice K. **The Utes.** Children's Press, 1998.

Fradin, Dennis. **From Sea to Shining Sea: Colorado.** Children's Press, 1993.

King, Virginia. **Sand.** Scholastic, 1993.

Taylor, Barbara. **Desert Life.** Dorling Kindersley, 1992

Organizations and Online Sites

The American Southwest
Great Sand Dunes
National Monument
*http://www.swlink.net/
~southwest/colo/sand/sand
.html*

An overview of the park's
natural wonders, plus
visitor information and
beautiful, clickable photos.

Friends of the Dunes
11500 Highway 150
Mosca, Colorado 81146
(719) 378-2312

A non-profit public support
group of the monument.
Members, from all fifty
states, work with the park
service to make visitors'
experiences at the dunes
meaningful and relevant.

**Great Sand Dunes
National Monument**
11999 Highway 150
Mosca, CO 81146-9798
http://www.nps.gov/grsa

The official website of the
park gives helpful tips for
your visit—recommended
clothing, nearby attrac-
tions, and special events
such as sand castle build-
ing contests.

Important Words

cornice an overhanging lip of sand, snow, or rock, occurring on a ridge

dune a hill or ridge of sand piled up by the wind

elevation height above the level of the sea

erosion to wear away by the action of water or wind

glacier a huge sheet of ice that moves slowly across land or mountains

grassland land on which the main plant forms are grasses

landmark something that marks a local place

migrate to move from one place to another

park ranger a person specially trained to protect the park

quicksand a deep mass of loose sand mixed with water

Index

Meet the Author

David Petersen lives in a cabin in Colorado's San Juan Mountains, a three-hour drive from the Great Sand Dunes, which he visits often. David is the author of numerous books of natural history for children and adults, and he has been writing for Children's Press since 1980. His True Books on America's national parks include *Bryce Canyon, Denali, Death Valley,* and *Petrified Forest.*